My Champion
And Other Inspirational Christian Poems

By Julie C. Gilbert

Love Science Fiction or Mystery?

Choose your adventure!
Visit: **http://www.juliecgilbert.com/**

For details on getting free stories.

Dedication:

To my friend Cara who always encouraged
me to rewrite and publish some of these.

To Barbara for inspiring the cover idea.

Special thanks to Timothy Sparvero for
illustrating some of the poems.

Table of Contents:

Introduction:

Dear Reader,

Although this is the third collection of inspirational Christian poetry, it contains the largest majority of the early poems.

The first two volumes are *Thin Black Road* and *Just Like You*.

The poems are specifically designed to be quick, easy reads with deep thoughts. Many are songs.

If you'd like a free copy of any of these for yourself or a friend, please email me at **devyaschildren@gmail.com**.

You can also email if you feel the need to share something, want to hear the song version, or would like some extra prayer.

Sincerely,

Julie C. Gilbert

1. My Champion

You are Lord in Heaven
Lord on this Earth.
Master and Maker,
King and Creator,
Father of all things,
And lover of my soul.

I have an enemy.
He knows how to hurt me.
He knows what I want to hear.
He knows how to twist my wants,
Make me think they're needs.
Help me drown out his voice.

Lord, be my victory,
Be my champion.
Show me Your glory.
Make me part of your story.
I want to know You better.
Open my ears, flood my mind.
Teach my heart to hear
You and only You.

2. On the Road of Life

Seems I've lost my way
On the road of life.
Don't know where to turn.
Couldn't turn around.
No going back now.
Biggest problem I see:
Too many paths before me.
Don't know which to choose,
Know I'll have to soon.
Cannot shake the feeling
Somehow, I've lost my way
On the road of life.
I know God's with me
I can hear Him say, "Trust me."
Funny how it's easy to swallow those words
When everything's steady
But knowing change is coming
Has me in an uproar.
Never was a big fan of change.
Still, I know God's with me.
Whenever I feel lost
I'll turn to Him
And find Him always there.

3. Who Will You Call?

Who will you call
When dark times come?
Who will you call
When hope fades away?
Who will you call your sole strength?
Who will you rest your soul in?
No matter what darkness may lie ahead
There is only one steady source of peace.

Call on Him from your knees
So that He may say,
"Rise, my child, I am here!
Find your rest in my arms.
Life may be hard, but I'm am stronger.
Won't you please call me?
Through me, the blind will see.
Through me, the lame will walk.
Do not let a lack of vision
Blind you from my power.
I am waiting to work great wonders
In and through you.
So, won't you please call me."

4. Unfair Tale

You may not believe in fairy tales
But listen to this unfair tale.
The King over everything had just one Son.
He condemned him to pain and death
Because you and I deserved to die.

You may say, "Never me.
I'm as good a person as can be."

That may be true, but haven't you heard?
Sinners and saints alike
Fall short of perfection.
If the story ended there
It'd be quite the tragedy,
But God found a way to set us free.

Jesus's death and sacrifice
Paved the way to paradise.

Now, one and all are invited
To claim new life, hope, and peace,
To claim their place in this family,
To become true royalty.

5. Fair
(For Chrissy)

When the pain in my head
Just won't go away,
What can I say?
Hallelujah. Hallelujah. Hallelujah.

The devil would like me to believe
The pain won't ever end.
The devil would like me to believe
Nobody cares for me.

When I hear these bold-faced lies
I can only drown them out
With a chorus from my soul:
Hallelujah. Hallelujah. Hallelujah.

We were never promised fair
This side of Heaven.
Quite honestly, we can't afford fair,
For it means all stand condemned.

Our Father in Heaven determined long ago
Life wouldn't be fair.
There would be relief through Jesus Christ.
Hallelujah. Hallelujah. Hallelujah.

6. To the Captive

Though you're a captive
And you may never hear my prayer,
I will pray, night and day,
God pours peace into your soul.

Love carried you far from home to a
Place and people you do not know.
Though I've never met you
I know the more you learn
The more you love.
Don't give up hope.
For we need to hear
The life lessons learned living over there.

Your fate lies in higher hands.
I will pray, night and day,
Cooler heads prevail and one day,
This will be a happy tale.

7. Chains are Gone

Jesus sought me though I fled Him
Day and night, he whispered truth.
Though no words ever touched my ears,
My heart clearly heard Him say:
"Come, dear child, come home.
I am waiting with open arms.
Don't you know the chains are gone?
They are vanquished by my love.
Can't you taste the sweet, free grace?"

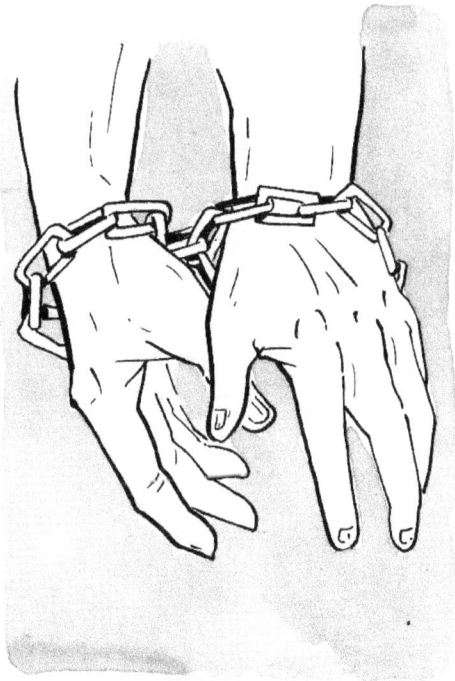

8. More Alive

When the skies are gray,
The grass looks a little greener.
When the skies are gray,
Smiles are a little warmer.
When the skies are gray,
Flowers shine a little brighter.
When the skies are gray,
Everything looks more alive!

The same holds true in my life.
When the skies are gray,
Many things that didn't impress me
Suddenly look better, brighter,
Full of hope I need.
When the skies are gray,
I cling to hope found in Christ.
This hope turns into peace
And I begin to feel more alive!

9. Place for Peace

There is a song deep inside
I must give release.
It's more like a cry:
O God, Why?
Why do these things happen?
Why can we not see the pain
That dwells in young minds?
They cry out in so many ways,
Yet we're blinded by the day to day.
They slip right through silently,
Then suddenly they're gone,
Faded like the last note of a song.

There is a place to find peace,
To find true release for all that pain.
Rest in God, weary ones.
You may think it's so easy
For me to say such things,
But I only know what I know
Because I've been where you are,
Lost and bound by fears.

10. Jesus, Father, God

Jesus, Father, God, and Holy King
Bless me, Lord, in everything.

Help me deal with all my pride.
I need you on my side.

Give me the right words to say.
I need strength for this day.

I want the world to see,
Christ Jesus shining in me.

I cannot make it on my own,
So I lay myself before your throne.

Jesus, Father, God, and Mighty King
Bless me, Lord, in everything.

11. Prayer Tonight

This is my prayer tonight:
Lord, teach me wrong from right,
Teach me what you want for me.
I will try to learn,
To read, to teach, and to discern.
Give me directions and I will go far.
Promises I break,
Mistakes that I make,
Are washed away by your blood.
Lord, haunt my every thought,
Help run this life you bought.

12. What I Love about My God

What I love about my God
Is that He loves me
More than I can see,
More than I could ever fathom.

What I love about my God.
Is that things on Earth
And things in Heaven
Obey Him.

What I love about my God
Is that He's everywhere.
He's always there.
He never fails.

What I love about my God
Is that He loves me
More than I can see,
More than I could ever fathom.

13. What's a Friend For

I see you look a little down today.
I hate to see you this way.
I hardly know what to say.

Cast your cares at the foot of the cross,
And as you wait on the Lord, talk to me.
What's a friend for, but to share your pain?
What's a friend for, but to keep you sane?
Now and always.

God's always there, and He always cares.
God's always there, and He never fails.
Still, He gave you friends to hold your hand.
He gave you friends to help you stand,
Through good and bad times.

14. God is There

God is there.
When everything is going right,
And life is good,
God is there.

God is there.
When your child is sick,
And you can't pay the bills,
God is there.

God is there.
When hope fades away,
And all you have is tears,
God is there.

God is there.
When you reach your goals,
And fulfill your dreams,
God is there.

15. Which Will it Be?

You must ask yourself
Which will it be?
During the easy times
It's easy to believe
That you'll always believe.
But during the hard times
Will your faith stand up?
Will you have the faith
To stand up for your faith?

16. One Soul at a Time

Lord God have mercy.
Shine down in glory.
Light up this world
One soul at a time.

Fill us with love for the lost ones.
Tune our spirits to hear
Cries for mercy.
You know what burdens
Lay heavy on hearts and minds.
Give us strength to break every chain.
Hopelessness. Helplessness.
Fear, pain, and loss too deep for words.
Take it away. Far, far away.
Replace it tenfold with hope
and peace too deep for words.

Lord God have mercy.
Shine down in glory.
Light up this world
One soul at a time.

No darkness can stand
Where your words are heard.
So, fill our voices with your praise.
We'll tear down the walls
Surrounding the lost ones
And call them to come home.
Fill us with boldness.
Fill us with brightness.
Use us to light up this world
One soul at a time.

17. Darkest Night

May the peace of God rest deep in you,
So you will walk on through this pain.
What words can cover for such a loss?
We've heard it all before.
Pain fades with time.
Heavy loss means lots of love.

Though I have been there before
And walked on through,
I remember asking God.
In the dark of night,
In the coldest parts of life,
Will I hear your voice whisper to my soul,
"Everything will be all right."?

With the advantage of hindsight
I see He was always there.
In my darkest night
In the coldest parts of life.
He lent strength and hope to my soul.

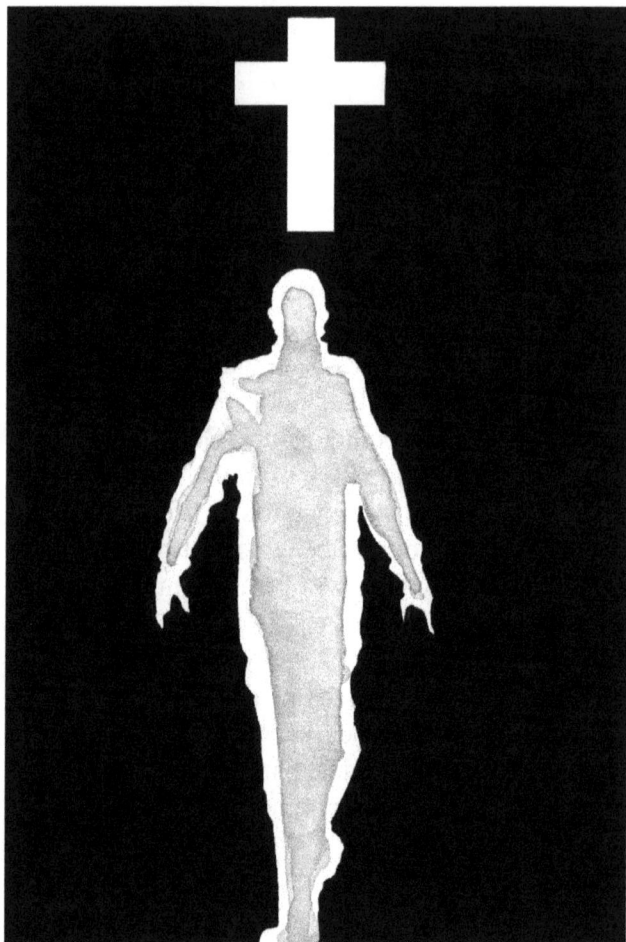

18. No Place for Fear

Life flies on by.
There's no stopping it.
Sometimes it's easy.
Enjoy those times,
For they may not last.
Do not fear,
For the Lord is near.
And when the Lord is near,
There's no place for fear.

19. Heavy Heart

Sometimes, I find my heart heavy
For I don't know how to reach you.
If you don't reach out to me,
I don't know what you need from me.

I can take no steps
If I don't know where to find you.
It's like shouting into dark
And hearing nothing,
Only to find out sometime later,
You were there the whole time,
Bound and gagged by helplessness,
Close enough to touch by hand,
But far away in mind and spirit,
And far beyond my reach.

Tell me, how can I reach you?
Is there some middle ground
We can safely tread?
Can we cross the distance
That lies between us?

Sometimes, I find my heart heavy
For I don't know how to reach you.
If you don't reach out to me,
I don't know what you need from me.

20. Set Me Free

Sweet Jesus, set me free.
Satan just won't let me be.
I'm a prisoner to my sin,
And I don't know where to begin.
I know I need you in my life.
Please help me through pain and strife.
Come into my heart today.
Let there be no further delay.

Sweet Jesus, you set me free,
Though Satan didn't want to let me be.
Thank you for everything.
It makes my soul want to sing.
You took my sins on you,
Washed me clean, and made me new.

.

.

21. Sure Promises

I know not what troubles you,
But keep the Lord in your sight
And everything will be all right.

Put your hope in the Lord.
Then come what may,
come what might,
He will help you through darkest night.
Each hard day will fade away.

Worry not to fail or fall
For He makes sure promises:
"Lean on me throughout your life.
I will walk beside you
And carry you when needed."

I don't know what tomorrow brings,
But I have learned to trust God.
He never ever fails or falls
All through trials I hear His calls,
"Trust me, my child."

22. I Lost Count
(For my mother)

On this Mother's Day,
I would like to say:
Thank you for everything you do.
Long ago, you took a child
And raised her to love the Lord.
I don't think there's a better
Gift you could give.
I know you didn't do this alone,
But this isn't his special day,
This is Mother's Day.

I lost count of the ways
God used you to touch me.
I lost count of the things
You taught me.
I lost count of the times
You picked me up, dried my tears,
And held me close after a fall.

I would try to count the ways,
But I wouldn't finish
For a thousand days.
All that's left to say is
Mom, I love you.

23. Day with God

Today, I spent the day with God.
I watched the clouds come down
And touch the mountains.
I saw the sun dance on tiny waves.
I think I needed this day.

Whether it was the hour of prayer,
The sunlit walk, the quiet time,
Or the chance to clear my mind …
I think I needed this day.

I spent the day with God.
No matter where my life will lead
I want to spend more days with Him.

24. On and On

I wanted a commander.
Someone to guide me.
Someone to tell me
Where to go, what to do,
Who to help, and how to act.
Instead, I got God.

How can I describe Him?
He's so much greater than I could imagine,
He is loving, kind, majestic,
Magnificent, glorious, perfect,
Holy, honorable, and beautiful,
Mighty, awesome, and gracious.
I could go on and on.

If I used every word mankind made,
I would barely begin to describe Him.

God has many roles to fulfill.
He is Master, Creator, Life-giver, Savior,
Hero, Father, Friend, and Teacher,
Counselor and Comforter,
Peacemaker, Judge and Healer.
Once again, I've only begun.
I could go on and on.

25. Always Safe

You know I have an active imagination
Because you gave it to me.
It is a source of endless joy,
As it takes me far away.
But at times, it is a source of worry
Because I can clearly picture
Everything going wrong.
Through it all, I will remember:
I am safe in Your arms.
I am safe until You let me go.
Since that day will never come,
I will always be safe.

Though I make many mistakes,
You never stop loving me.
You know every time I fall away
Yet You draw me close anyway.
Through hard times
I will always remember:
I am safe in Your arms.
I am safe until You stop loving me.
Since that day will never come,
I will always be safe.

26. Tell Me I Am Silly

Tell me I am silly.
Tell me I worry too much.
Tell me my fears are only dreams.
See, I fear not for me,
But I worry for those I love.
My imagination likes to run wild.
It is a blessing and a curse.

Every unaccounted moment
Brings up fears that they'll die
And leave me all alone.
I know that's silly.
So, tell me I am silly.
Tell me I worry too much.
Tell me my fears are only dreams.

God, I beg You
Never let these fears come to pass.
Come be my peace of mind.
Tell me I am silly
Then post Your presence
As guard of my heart.

27. Melt Hearts

Do not fear
What the future holds.
Nothing can hold you captive
If you believe.

I believe:
Prayer can set wrongs to right,
Melt hearts made of stone,
And heal brokenness.

I believe:
Love, hope, and peace
Are treasures to cherish
When darkness, hardship, and heartache
Try to sink your spirits low.

28. Everybody Runs

Everybody runs. Everybody hides.
Everybody tries to say
It's not their fault.
But the truth remains:
Our sins are hard to miss.
Only God's love can save us.

Why do people run?
Why do people hide?
Why do people try to say
It's not their fault?
When the truth remains:
God's love is hard to miss.

O Lord, thank you for being
Patient with my wayward heart.
You whispered, "I love you."
Until I finally accepted
It as truth.

29. How Many Times?

I do not know
How many times
In this life
I will fail.

But I do know
That every time
I can return to the foot of the cross
And receive my redemption.

I will bring the broken pieces
Of my spirit to the Lord
And He will make me whole.

30. Blessings

I have food, friends, and family
Yet these pale in comparison
With the greatest gift:
God's Son.

I cling to hope for a bright future.
I must remember
Where the blessings come from.

Thank you, Father, for loving me,
Even before I drew a breath.
Thank you for the many blessings
That have made my life so grand!

31. Disappointment

Sometimes life sends me flying.
I'd be lying if I said this
Doesn't disappoint, but I understand
God's got something better in mind for me.
At this time, I just can't see
That future unfurled.

I'd be lying if I said this doesn't disappoint.
I wish I could see my future.
I wish decision-making was much easier.
Heck, while I'm at it,
I wish I never had another worry.
But that's not the way life works.
I am glad that I know God
For of the two of us
He's the one who knows what's going on.

When life sends me flying,
I can fly free and clear in mind,
Knowing He's ready to catch me,
Set me on my feet, and lead me by the hand.

32. Today's Rain

Nothing's really wrong today,
But rain's got my spirits down.
Rain makes the flowers grow,
But that doesn't make me like it.
It possesses a dark, dreary power
That bids me go to sleep.
At the same time, I find the soft
Splatter of rain versus ground, soothing.
Rain makes the grains grow
And that sort of makes me like it.
Thank God for the rain.

God made the rain.
Now, that makes me like it.
Rain pulls my spirits down,
But God pulls my spirits up.
Feeling down makes it easier
To sense God's presence.
The blessings outweigh the emotional low.
I'll thank God for the rain
Because it waters my soul today.

33. Safe Spot

I know I put it in a safe spot.
The only problem is that I
Do not remember where that is.
I know it's in a safe spot.
So safe, even I can't find it.
This is driving me crazy.
I've got to stop doing this
If I want to keep my nerves intact.

Too safe's gonna make me
Find it too late.
I know it's not the end of the world,
But it sure is irksome.
The thing I want to find
Is a little too safe for me.

34. Far Away Honor

All I want to do is worship the Lord
With prayers and deeds
And writings that please Him.

I want to let my mind
Conjure up worlds far away,
Where people encounter problems much
Like ours and discharge
Their duties honorably.

We've let honor and duty
Fall to the wayside,
But in worlds far away,
I can bring both back,
In flashes of light, and justice by might.

One day, honor will return to Earth,
For the end game's written:
God wins.
Choose whom to serve.

35. Rare Truth

God loves us.
This is one rare truth.
Christ died for us.
This is another rare truth.
Both are basic Christian knowledge.
I wish to speak on a third rare truth.

Quickly, we forget God is Holy.
We forget that He's always listening.
Often, we let our tongues rule us.
One minute, we're praising God,
And the next, we're cursing, like fools.
Our hearts are so fickle!

I wish I could say it was different for me,
But my heart also wanders.
I don't lack fervor,
But who and what I call master varies.
One minute, I'm serving God,
And the next, I'm serving self.

I wish I could grow out of this,
But I fear it shall always be
A wearying battle for me.

36. Content to be Content

There are a great many dreams
I wish to see come true.
But for now, I am content to be content.

That doesn't mean I won't
Fight for my dreams with
Prayers and deeds and writings on hope.

Though I am content to be content,
I'm more convinced than ever
I have a calling to fulfill.
Idle musings about where this will lead
And what the cost will be
Will never deter me for long.

When I feel weary, I will pray.
I will arm myself with knowledge.
I will practice to no end.
I will push myself to the edge
And cast myself over, knowing full well
I'll land in His arms and there I will be
Content to be content.

37. Blinders

Why are we not better off
Than in ages past?
Terrorists scare us. Vows mean nothing.
Murders are confined to page fifteen.
People do whatever they please.
In a time when morals
Get defined by individuals
There's a shortage of good.
Part of me wishes for the past
When people knew they were bad.
They were defiant in their sin,
But at least, they didn't rationalize.
Deluded people are hardest to reach.
"That's good for you but not for me,"
Is ten times more infuriating than
"Just leave me to my sin."
Lord, save us from self-imposed blinders.

38. Shadows of Change

I could tell you many a sad tale
Concerning the shadows of our past.
Tales of woe, darkness, pain,
Where our heroine's nearly slain.
Her beaten body draws our eyes,
Her broken spirit tugs our hearts,
Her overthrown mind, saddest of all,
Awakens pity pure and deep.
Why's this tale sound so real?
Could it be we've heard this before?
What good is sympathy if
Our minds can't fathom change?

Some were born to privilege
Yet remain blind to it.
You and I may agree to disagree
On a great many things,
But let us not waste time debating.
Those given much have much to give.
Sometimes, the best gift is an open heart.
What good is sympathy
If our minds can't fathom change?
Hear these tales, picture change,
Move your heart first, then the world.

39. God the Artist

Did you know God's an artist?
This world shows God's an artist.
Have you seen a baby,
Soft and sweet, full of life,
Made unique by God's hands?
Have you seen the ocean?
Heard the waves pound the surf,
Wondered where they come from?
Have you watched the sunset
From the heights of a mountain?
If you had then you'd know
God must be an artist.
Have you heard the birds
Sweetly summon the sun to shine?
Have you seen the forests
Clothed in cheerful colors?
I could go on forever.
So many sights and sounds declare
God must be an artist.

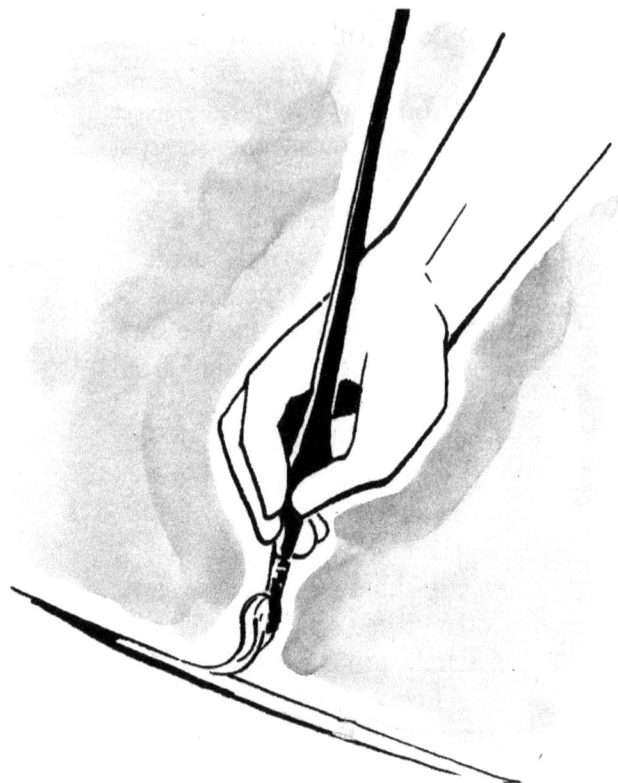

40. Hundred Percent

Idols come in many forms.
If something consumes your mind
And isn't God, it could be sin.
See, it ain't easy being pure.
See, it ain't easy measuring up.
There's a hundred percent failure rate.
Where's the hope in that?

There's always hope.
There's a hundred percent certainty
Jesus Christ died to set us free
From sin's sinister shackles.
Won't you claim this freedom?
Live your life striving to be good.
Fight evil within and without
With all you are.
Don't be surprised when you fall.
If you surrender this fallen you
God is ready to work on your heart.

41. I've Gained

I had somebody ask for my help today.
It was a most unusual request.
I forget her exact words,
But the essence of the message was:
"Pray for my friend,
You do not know her,
But worse, she doesn't know our Lord.
This is a tough time of transition
Would you pray for my friend?
Would you reach out to her?
She doesn't know our Lord."

Well, what could I say?
"Of course, I will pray.
I hope God will help me find your friend.
I see she is on your heart."

What kind of friendship
Forms such compassion?
I think I want that.
I think I've gained something
Better than gold today.
I've gained a friend I may never meet.
I've gained new reason to send up prayers.
I've gained so much, now it's time to give.

42. Lasts, Firsts, and Changes
(college graduation)

Now that I know the next step
The burden of waiting is finally gone.
It's a year for lasts, firsts, and changes.
I do not do well with these.
Still, I hope in hard times
Of waiting, not knowing, or changing
My faith will shine brighter
And stronger than all my impatience.
It's a time for lasts, firsts, and changes
What a wonderful time to live.

There is something extra cheerful
In the sunshine this time of year.
How I wish these days
Could go on forever!
Since I cannot stop the lasts,
Firsts, and changes,
I will trust in and praise God
For He has all things well in hand.

43. Simply Everywhere

There's a world between you and me.
I may not know what assails your mind
And though I've never felt the pain you do,
I'll cross this distance
On the wings of my prayers
And I'll hold you in my mind
Like one holds a crying child.
In Christ, the distance fades away
For the One we serve is
Neither here nor there, simply everywhere.

There's a world between you and me.
Though it seems the struggle may never end
Thought you'd like to know
How much you inspire.
Not by your strength but simply faith.
I see my Master in the works of your mind
And I want to join that work.
So, I'll cross this distance
On the wings of my prayers
And together we'll praise the One
Who is neither here nor there,
Simply everywhere.

44. Dream Meaning

Am I dreaming?
If I'm dreaming, leave me sleeping,
I find I like this pretty dream.
I saw something I only ever saw
In my mind come to life today.

If I'm dreaming leave me sleeping,
I find I like this pretty dream.
As I touch this dream,
Hold it in my hands,
I'll praise the Lord Most High
For He gave me this dream.

Now that it's come true
I'll pray His blessings
Rain down on me,
For only in the Lord
Was this dream ever
Meant to mean anything.

45. More than Silver

I see you wear a cross,
A tiny piece of silver,
Hanging from a chain.
Do you wear it as a charm,
Or does it mean more?
Jesus Christ, God made flesh,
The only one to fully conquer death
Made the cross so much more than silver.
His love manifested in grace
Leads lost souls to life.

The cross can be
A tiny piece of silver
Hanging from a chain
Or it can mean so much more.
Life in Christ may be
As painful as living without
But His life gives us hope
That though the towers of today
May still be fragile,
The cross is so much more than silver.

46. Crucify Him

Deep in a dream
I heard myself scream,
"Crucify Him!"

I woke with a start,
Stricken in heart,
Surprised to find my eyes
Wet with tears.

I silently begged sleep to return,
Knowing it was not meant to be.
I needed to think.
The dream haunted me deeply.

Finally, I realized that every time
He gave me directions,
I defiantly cry, "Make me!"

I might as well be crying,
"Crucify Him!"

With this realization fresh in my mind,
I made my peace with God,
Falling into a deep, sweet sleep
Before my smile faded.

47. Sands of Time

Come watch the sands of time
Sweep on by.
Though sense says
Hold on to all those dear
We face this journey without fear.

Come watch the sands of time
Sweep on by.
All good sense inquires:
Why cling to fruitless pride
When time may not be on your side?

Come watch the sands of time
Sweep on by.
Truth be told boldly.
There may be substance to fears.
Tears may pave the way through years.

Come watch the sands of time
Sweep on by.
Let not sorrows rule
For hope will always remain.
Though things will never be the same.

48. Rose on My Grave

I have seen too many people
Pass from this life
To think I'll escape unscathed.
Life can change in a moment
Or end in a flash.
While we're on this topic
I have some questions for you.
Will you place a rose on my grave?
Will you be among those I count a friend?
Just one rose placed on my grave
Will mean somebody knows.
For not much in this life I fear
But one thought can haunt me
I fear of fading into dark
Alone.

49. His Mighty Hand
(For Areck)

The work of His mighty hand
Shines through you
Your servant's heart has served
Many people very well.
You may never know
What heart's you have touched
With a simple smile or well-placed word.

His mighty hand rests upon you
May it guard you from disappointment.
May it carry you through all manner of pain
To the day you will gain
Crowns to cast at His feet
When we will sing glory to the One King
Whose mighty hand rests upon you.

He has done great things with your soul.
We will watch and wait with great hope
For life's play to move forward.
We will watch and wait to see
Where His mighty hand will take you
And what great things He can do
Through one willing servant's heart.

50. We Cried Mercy and God Delivered
(For Bernadette)

As our hearts crumble
With deep-seated sorrows,
We take hope in a promise.
God knows all our tomorrows.

We cried mercy and God delivered.
It was not the way
We would have wished it.
So, now we cry for mercy:
Great God, deliver us from this pain.

Though we weep
For the one who fell asleep,
Someone wise once told me
One day we will see her
And even hear her say:
"What took you so long
To come home?"

Long before we thought to cry mercy,
God healed the world through his only Son
So that we who cry mercy
May know true peace through Him.
We can take hope in this promise:
Every time we cry mercy
God will deliver.

51. You are Royalty
(For Kaiwen)

I've known you less than a thousand days,
Seen you less than half of that.
It's been a privilege to know you this long.
Though I could do without some hardships
I would not change one day of my life.
Hopefully, you can say the same.
My hope and prayer for you is this:
Let God work His will in you.
Day in and day out if you listen
You will hear Him speak quiet words.

No one knows the hour or day
Our Lord will come to claim His own,
Go forth and seize upon
Every chance to shine His words
In thought and deed.

Indeed, if you let Him wholly reign in you,
No trial, no hardship, nothing at all
Can hold you back.
There will be nothing your spirit lacks.
When something tries to bring you low
Remember who you are.
You're a child of God,
You are royalty.

52. Plans God has for You
(For Taylor)

You may not know exactly
What plans God has for you,
But you know inside it's true:
God's got a plan that will unfold
Like a story untold
When the time is right.
Hold Him in your sight.

When you leave this place
Please hold a space
In your heart and mind
For those left behind.

We do not know exactly
What plans God has for you,
But we know inside it's true:
You're in good hands.
No matter where you land
No matter what you face
No matter how you run this race.

Cling to truths learned here.
Face the future without fear,
Knowing none of life's demands
Can ever steal you from God's hands.

53. Beautiful Reflection
(For Cristina)

When I think of you
The word *beauty* comes to mind,
In and out I find
You're a beautiful reflection of God.

Cool, calm, and quiet sometimes,
More often bursting with passion,
May your love of life always serve Christ.
Continue to be a beautiful reflection of God.

Many a day passed by
I regret I did not try
To know you better.
You're a beautiful reflection of God.

Never lose that fire inside
Nor attempt to hide
The gifts God has lavished upon you.
You're a beautiful reflection of God.

There will be days
Set against you in many ways.
When doubts try to take you low
Remember who you are
And who you reflect inside.

Nothing at all can forever claim
Someone sealed in His name.

54. Nothing and Nobody

Heard there was young
Woman ready to end her life
Though it's barely begun.
Seems it's a story told
Too many times these days,
So many times, it kind of gets old.

As I get older
My heart gets colder
I must remember to pray:
"Lord, melt this ice away."

I've been thinking kind of hard.
Think I'm ready to provide
Conclusions:
When it comes right down to the core
Everybody needs nothing and nobody
But the Lord God Almighty
On their side.

55. With My All

When I look at you
Fear for the future
Fades, for then I remember
Everything from that first September
To the present and far beyond
Has passed just as God planned.

You are beautiful, intelligent, unafraid
Of giving your time and talent, unpaid.
The works of your mind and heart
Will be sorely missed as you depart.
I could go on and on
About the many ways you're a paragon.
It's been a pleasure to watch you grow
I wonder where God will have you go.

Please remember to always pray:
"Dear God, lead me day by day
Take my mind and mold it.
Fill me with Your Spirit!
Give me ears to hear Your call
To pray and praise You with my all."

56. As the End Draws Near
(For Victor)

Not so long in the past
You asked me for a song.
At the time, I could not
Grant your request.

As the end of your time here draws near,
I feel drawn to say farewell
In a way you'll remember well.

We've heard the songs
That draw you nearer to God.
May that gift born deep inside you
Never fail to praise His name.

As the end draws near,
It's my hope and prayer
That each of us learns how to praise
God with heart, mind, and soul.

May it be that every day
Our hearts rise to say:
*Here I am, Lord, take my spirit
Make me more like You today.*

57. If You Only Knew
(For Mark)

Did you know?
Nearly every word said
Could be turned into a song
If you only knew how to
Make it work for you.

Any thought, any phrase,
Any feeling locked inside
Can be given new form.
If you only knew how to
Make it work for you.

To some extent such a thing
Can't be learned in a class.
You must learn it from life.
Everything, good or ill,
Holds a lesson inside
If you only knew how to
Make it work for you.

Every day take some time to pray:
"Dear Lord God, help me find
Every word, every phrase,
Every feeling You want unlocked.
Take this gift placed in me
Use it for Your glory.
May my only goal
Be to bring You praise."

58. Nobody Knows
(For Alyssa)

One could hardly call you shy.
I can't remember a day gone by
When a smile has failed to grace
Your lovely face.
Did you know your strong
Spirit could pull people along,
Out of the depths of despair
By letting them know you care?

Nobody knows what tomorrow may
Bring your way:
Trials or triumphs or unknown pains.
Seems sometimes we keep sane
By pushing all thoughts away
And simply living day by day.
I know you know you need not fear
But I feel I should be clear:
God knows your heart, mind, and soul
And what you need to keep whole.

Praise God in good times
When things works out fine.
Other days, cling to this truth:
Life may not always be smooth
But God is God through it all.
Listen closely, you'll hear His call:
"Reach those headed for a hungry grave
It was for them I died to save."

59. Charge to Class of 2009

You may leave and never look back,
But I hope you will not lack
For fond memories of all you've done,
Though your life has barely begun.
Every end births something new.
There's not much else to do,
But reflect upon the things you know.
Prepare to enter the world and sow
Seeds of truth and seeds of light,
Set the world's wrongs to right.
Moment by moment, day by day
Find the will inside to pray.
Lord, your grace knows no end.
Give me wisdom to defend
This fragile faith.
I need strength to cling to what is dear
To your heart and to your mind.
Help me help others find
This peace surpassing all knowledge
For such is my privilege
As a child of the One King.
There are countless other reasons to sing
Your praises all day long.
May every act for good become a song
Of praise to You.

60. Charge to Class of 2010

It will long be my fervent prayer
That you take life with a care.
Guard your eyes and ears
Lest the things that slip by lead to tears.
I know it is easy
To think *never me,*
But the world's whispers and shouts
Are enough to sow many doubts.
So many innocent minds walk out that door
Unguarded and wind up spiritually poor.

It will long be my fervent prayer
That you take life with a care.
Never thought I'd be back.
Found my life on a far-away track,
Not necessarily right or wrong,
Just that I found I didn't belong
In that place, in that time.
In the end it worked out fine
Because God had a plan for my life,
One great enough to carry me through strife.

It will long be my fervent prayer
That you take life with a care.
Trust the Lord in everything
So at the end of time you can hear Him say,
"Well done, my good and faithful servant."

61. Be Brave, Be Bold
(For the Class of 2011)

You will go far in this life.
Whether your role is to change
A thousand lives, ten times that, or only one,
May the Lord's hand of mercy
Reach through your life and shower love
On those who surround you.

You won't be perfect, not by far.
We were not asked to be Christ,
Only to let Christ be Christ in us.

As you leave this place,
Be brave, be bold.
Hold tightly to the truth.
It may not seem epic
From where we're standing,
But we are locked in a battle
For the souls of mankind.
So be brave, be bold,
Hold onto this truth:
In the end God wins.

62. He Knows Your Heart

When you're weary, without rest,
When you're ready to fall apart
In a moment's time,
Sing praise to the Holy One,
Sing praise to the only one
Who knows your heart
Better than you do.

He knows what fears haunt your dreams.
He knows each tear you shed in secret.
No motive you have ever held
Deep within your mind
Can change the simple facts:
He died to rise to love you more.
He died to rise to save your soul.
He died to rise to give you rest.

When you're weary, rest in Him.
When you're ready to fall apart
Sing praise to the Holy One,
Sing praise to the only one
Who knows your heart
Better than you do.

63. Meant to Say

(For my grandmother, Miriam Smith)

Captured in a child's mind
There exists a pretty picture.
I remember many stairs, a fancy church,
Afternoons spent outside climbing tires.
Ten summer visits blending into one.

Do you remember the shy smile I wore
When my heights triumphed over yours?
I think you shrank more than I grew,
But I'm allowed some delusions.
I digress...
I really meant to say,
"I wish I had ten thousand words
To express how I love you
But why waste words when three will do?
I wish I had ten thousand years
To expound on how I love you.
You are a precious person
I'm blessed to know."

64. What If

Sometimes you come upon
A place to choose a new path.
A glance down the past road
Leaves you wondering what if …
If only you could have known
Where every road would lead.

A peek down the current choices
Leaves you wondering what if …
the future whispered its secrets.
Make sure these "what ifs"
Don't leave you paralyzed,
Afraid to move on,
Unable to go back and start again.

If you could borrow courage
Enough to take one step
You would find the future easier to claim.
You would find some peace
And solace in this knowledge:
No matter where you have been,
What you have done,
Who or what has hurt you along the way,
The next step belongs to you.

65. Walk Free

Father, Prince of Peace,
Lend me strength to release,
This need to control my fate.
Help me to wait well.
I sometimes wonder why
You who placed the stars so high
Would descend to this place
To save a fallen race.
A child, a king, a ransom.
That's a steep price to pay.

If we listen, we can hear your call:
"Come sinners, one and all.
Come near, dear child.
Come claim your inheritance
Leave nothing to chance.
Darkness, pain, and fear
Have no more place here.
Your debt is paid in full.
Walk free.
Taste true life as it should be."

66. Our Lady

Have you come to see our lady?
She stands next to the sea.
How many have come to see our lady?
Countless strangers are inspired by her.
She hails from distant shores
Standing for timeless values.
She holds words of freedom in one hand
A bright torch to light the way.
Have you come to see our lady?
For a hundred years or more
She has graced our shore
Offering hope to desperate thousands
Wandering here to begin new lives.
As you gaze at her strong face
Let your worries wash away.
Though heartache may follow,
Hold onto hope.
When you're weary think of our lady.
Have you come to see our lady?

67. Angel in Disguise
(For my friend, Jenny)

Anyone ever tell you you're an angel?
Maybe not a real one but real enough
To the thousands who see
Christ's love in you.
You can hide it with humility
But it shines ever brighter with every prayer.
Your small acts of kindness go a long way.
Though others may not see your deeds,
They are tiny little seeds
Sewn into the hearts of the needy.
Your well-timed smiles and gentle spirit
Have carried wounded souls
To the only source of lasting peace.
There's hardly a greater victory.
That makes you a hero.
That makes you an angel in disguise.
Of course, not a real one
But real enough to the lives you touch.

68. Heart Cry

There was a time in my life
When all was simply strife.
You don't know how far I've come
To find safety and true love.

How was I to know
You were here all the time
Waiting and watching,
Hungry for my heart and soul?

It may sound trite,
But now I clearly see
I was not completely me
Until I knew you.

I feel I could face anything
Now that I know you
Will watch and wait,
Keep me safe from true dark.

Before this very moment,
I felt quite the lonely captive,
But here with you holding me
I at last feel truly free.

69. The Proud Angel's Fall

He was the most beautiful of all the angels.
And he had power to be sure.
Then, one day, he said, "I should be God."
And a third of the angels agreed.
He was cast from Heaven.
Now, he is lord over Hell.

There's a lesson to be learned here.
No matter how beautiful you are,
No matter how powerful you are,
Always remember who created beauty,
And who gave you power.

Take pride in working for the Lord,
But always remember God is God,
Only He has the right to reign
Over everything.

70. Bound

Among the many mistakes that I have made
The most painful is falling in love with you.
Thought I could change you.
Thought I could claim you for the truth.
I see I lied to me.

I know you love me
But my heart is not free.
I'm bound by belief to serve the Lord.
If only I'd listened to His teachings.
Maybe I'd save us all this heartache.

I know you love me
But your heart is not free.
You're bound to the world.
The closer you draw
To the gods of this world.
The farther you'll be from me.

Don't you see we serve different masters?
I disobeyed mine; look where it got me.
I'll make it right now.
It's the most painful thing to me
But I know I must flee,
Before my heart is bound to you again.

71. The Mask
(A poem based on Nadia Ayers)

I am a prisoner to my thoughts.
Who can free me?
I am trapped in a tower.
There is no entrance,
No exit, no escape.
Fear and frustration build up.

I wear a smile as a mask.
Can you read the pain I feel?
My family means everything.
My siblings and I have many Gifts.
We can and will change the world.
Not much world-changing
Happens peacefully.
Some will hunt us.
Some will fear us.
Some will hate us for no reason.

I wear a smile as a mask.
Can you read the pain I feel?
I can read strangers' thoughts
But I cannot control hearts or minds.
Love will have to rule.
My siblings know me best.
The future's uncertain,
But my loyalty will always
Belong to family.

72. Sense of Death

How could the king
Abandon us by his death?
Where are the honors due the fallen queen?
This place reeks of death.
I need no other clues or accounts.
A sense of death surrounds you,
Poisoning the air.

Few truly know the truth.
Fewer still are brave enough
To speak out against this injustice.
A sense of death surrounds you,
Poisoning the air.

It's no wonder they keep their silence
They must have more regard
For their life than I have mine.
I cannot keep silent.
Kill me if you will.
A sense of death surrounds you,
Poisoning the air.

I will add my voice to the whispers
Speaking against the wrongs done here.
A sense of death surrounds you,
Poisoning the air.
Can you feel it closing in?

73. Carry the Message

I went to the Captain and announced,
"I'm tired of being on the sidelines!
I want to be of use in these hard times.
Captain, please give me another task,
For I am tired of watching others.
They gain glory and honor,
While I tend their horses!"

The Captain nodded and said,
"That is the task I have set for you,
But if you wish more, consider this,
Every task is worthy of honor,
And glory comes from how you perform.
Go! Carry the message to the troops."

I merely nodded, sad and confused.
I went for a walk deep in thought.
"How is a stable boy as good as a soldier?
It is not fair that we are at war …"

Then, I walked past the wounded tent.
One man lay on his cot and prayed,
"Bless the Captain for this task,
Allow me to fulfill my duty well."

I waited for the soldier to finish.
Curious, I asked,
"Sir, what is your task?"

He smiled and said,
"I am to encourage the soldiers,

And write them letters, lad."

"Is there honor in that?" I wondered.

The soldier looked at me kindly.
"Lad, we have peace and rest,
But many are not so lucky.
We have good news to share.
Others must know that we still care.
To sharing this is a glorious task.
There are many to hear,
But few to carry the letters."

That day, I received my commission.
Now, I too carry the letters
To those hard at work.
There are even missives
For those who have not heard.
My new task is to tell of the King
And encourage the soldiers.
"The enemy had fled in many places."

74. Those Days

I remember the days
When we walked the halls of heaven,
Hand in hand, heart in heart,
Our minds as one.
Do you remember those days?
Days of exploring the land.
Days of creating from dawn 'til dusk.
Everything new, everything good.
Tell me you remember those days.

Tell me you remember …
The day we discovered the meaning of life.
The day we shared love for the first time.
The day we made the sun stand still
Just because we could.
Carefree days, careless days.
What would I give to return to those days?
The could have beens,
The should have beens,
They haunt me.
I think a season or two slipped by
While I did nothing but cry
For what we had, what we lost,
And everything in between.
Do you remember those days?

75. Heart of a Hero

Tears fall and purge my eyes.
My heart aches such that I must speak.
Woe to the maid in love with a hero.
There lies a hero near unto death,
And here I flee as he bid.
Curse my promise to live.
Part of me prays Spirit let him live
One more day, one more night,
Part of me wonders, would it matter?
For such is the heart of a hero
To throw himself in death's way.
It was my life he saved this day.
I know for sure, had he lived
He'd be right back in this war
For he had the heart of a hero.
Even in death he'll live on
For love bids me take his fight.
The heart of hero must never die,
And it never will so long as love is a word.
For such is the core of hero's heart.

76. First Half of a Moment

Sunny days and starlight,
Smiles and faces of friends held dear,
Are locked within my mind,
Bright and clear.
I am terrified that one day
They will fade away.

The last things I saw:
A red light, a black car,
Flying glass, and my own hands
Will be forever blazed into my mind.

People complain their lives are so busy.
They just want to slow down,
Take a breath, and start over.
Be careful what you wish for,
For everything can change
In the first half of a moment.

The last things I saw:
A red light, a black car,
Flying glass, and my own hands
Will be forever blazed into my mind.

I wanted a change of pace,
But this is crazy.
How could I have known that
In the first half of a moment,
In the space between heartbeats,
My vision would be forever
Confined to what I remember?

All is darkness and cold loneliness,
Wish I could see the faces around me.
Please don't cry.
It hurts enough as is.
All is strange and new,
So daily, I'll replay the scenes:
Sunny days and starlight,
Smiles, and faces of friends held dear.

77. Adern's Strength

(Published in *Reshner's Royal Ranger*)

Nehkermah stenmielsto
Keqwirco seikero.
Sehnomfreh.
Sehstimorea.
Nehnqwirm seikero.
Sehnawbon.
Sehnomorikan.
Nehnqwirm seikero.

No fiery danger striking near my heart
Can kill or conquer, when I have love.
See how it floods me.
See how my strength grows.
Nothing can conquer me, when I have love.
See how it binds every wound.
See how my strength rises from ashes.
Nothing can conquer me, when I have love.

78. My Heart Belongs in the Mountains

(Based on *Reshner's Royal Ranger*)

See where the mountains reach up
And kiss the sky,
That's where you'll find me.
My heart belongs in the mountains.
Though I wasn't born there,
So many years went by that I
Couldn't imagine life anywhere but there,
Yet the more I'm around you
The easier it is to forget
My heart belongs in the mountains.
Every time I close my eyes
I can clearly picture you,
Your ice blue eyes, warm smile, rich laugh—
I must forget or go crazy!
How many times must I remind me?
My heart belongs in the mountains!
I know you know I love you,
And I've felt the same from you.
Is it enough to cross the distance?
Maybe one day you'll come find me.
Just go where the mountains reach up
And kiss the sky
That's where you'll find me.

79. Beautiful Land

(Based on *Reshner's Royal Guard*)

Beautiful land,
You hold much power over me.
See, you have my heart and soul
Just as you have my body
Locked here by gravity.
My dreams go no higher than your peaks,
No farther than your seas.
Once or twice they brushed the stars,
But always my thoughts returned home.

Wish I could spend my days and nights
Wandering hills, fields, and forests.
Duty may keep me palace-bound,
But one day I'll climb a mountain
Or walk by the sea for hours,
Listening to it whisper
Or rage as the case may be.
Until that day, dreams will do.

Beautiful land,
Do I love you because you're home,
Or are you home because I found
Love here?

80. You Make Life All Right
(Inspired by *Reshner's Royal Guard*)

Sleep well, little princess.
Dawn will come soon.
Don't you know? You bring hope to my life!

May the night hold peaceful dreams.
May the morning's light shining on you
Bring a smile to your eyes.
When those blue gems light from within
Worry fades away.
Sleep well, little princess.
Don't you know? You make life all right!

Storms may be coming.
The thought of wind leveling
Land from shore to shore
Almost sinks my spirits low.
Then, I remember you
And worry fades away.
Sleep well, little princess.
Don't you know? You make life all right!

War may be coming.
The thought of chaos reigning here
Almost drowns my soul with despair.
Then, I remember you and worry fades away.
Sleep well, little princess.
Don't you know? You make life all right!

81. He Leapt for Joy

When Elizabeth heard Mary's voice
The baby within leapt for joy.
He leapt for joy
Because he knew
The one who walked his way
Would one day bear a son,
And that boy would be
The Savior of the world.

He leapt for joy
Because he could do no less
In the presence of the King.

Filled with the Spirit
Elizabeth cried out,
"Blessed are you among women
Blessed be the child you will bear!
But why am I so favored,
That the mother of my Lord
Should come to me?
As soon as the sound of your greeting
Reached my ears
The baby within leapt for joy."

He leapt for joy
Because he could do no less
In the presence of the King.

82. No Body

As was foretold long ago,
Our Lord was cruelly crucified,
And so, the grave would be satisfied.
After the deed was done,
They laid his body down,
Deep down in a garden tomb.

Three days later,
As the sun rose on a new week,
Women took spices to the tomb,
But they found no body.
Just some strangers dressed in clothes
that gleamed like lightning.

They found no body.
Just some strangers with a crazy claim:
"He has risen."

You can believe me
Or walk away,
But you can't change
What happened that day.
They found no body.

Thank You for Reading:

I hope you enjoyed reading this third Christian Inspirational poetry collection. While reviews are awesome, let's do something different. If something in here touched you in anyway, share it with somebody else.

What does that mean? God has given everybody gifts. If you paint, paint. If you sing, sing. If you draw, draw. If you bake, bake, and so forth. Put the phrase or title or even a whole poem (if applicable) on your labor of love and use it to bless somebody.

It does not have to be shared on social media, and in some cases, it shouldn't. However, if you do, use #MTPchallenge if you choose to share via social media and tag me if you like. I'm on Facebook, Twitter, Instagram, and Mewe.

If you'd like to try some fiction, check out my website (**juliecgilbert.com**). Many stories can be experienced in ebook, paperback, or audiobook. I highly recommend the audiobooks as I've worked very hard to hire talented people to bring these stories to life.

Hop on the **newsletter** if you want to keep up with life and new release news.
(https://www.subscribepage.com/n7e8l8)

Sincerely,
Julie C. Gilbert